END TIMES BIBLE PROPHECY:
My Personal Sermon Notes

by
Dave Williams

First Printing 1991

ISBN: 0-938020-39-0
MOUNT HOPE MINISTRIES
Copyright ©1991   David R. Williams
Printed in the United States of America

TABLE OF CONTENTS

LESSON 1:
Laying Some Groundwork in Bible Prophecy

TEXT: Matthew 24

I.   **THE DISCIPLES ASKED ESSENTIALLY THREE QUESTIONS (v. 3)**
   A. When?

   B. What Will Be the Signs of Your Second Coming?

   C. What Will Be the Signs of the End of the Age?

II. **DEFINITIONS**
   A. END OF THE AGE = End of Church Age (at Rapture)

   B. SECOND COMING = The Return of Christ at the End of the 7-Year Tribulation Period

III. **OLIVET DISCOURSE (Matthew 24:1-25:46)**
   A. Adds Some Details and Ties Together the Books of Daniel and Revelation.

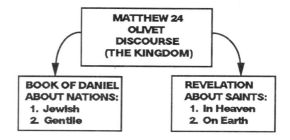

V. **MATTHEW CHAPTER 24 — COMPLETE OVERVIEW**
A. Verse 3 — The Questions

B. Verses 4-8 — The First Sign (before The Rapture of the Church)

C. Verses 9-14 — Complete Overview of the 7-Year Tribulation

D. Verses 15-26 — Especially to the Jews During the Tribulation Period
   1. Note: v. 16 "which be in Judea" (Jews).
   2. Note: v. 20 "neither on the Sabbath day" (This wouldn't matter to Gentiles; only Jews).

E. Verses 27-28 — Mode of Christ's Return
   1. He will come from the sky, not from the desert or elsewhere.
   2. He will be the same Jesus, not a different person.
   a. See also Acts 1:10-11

F. Verses 29-30 — After the Great 7-Year Tribulation at the Last War Known as Armageddon.

G. Verse 31 — Post-Tribulation Rapture
   1. Not the same as the Rapture of the Church in I Thessalonians 4:14-18.
   2. This post-tribulation rapture will gather the ones who accepted Christ during the tribulation and survived.

H. Verses 32-35 — Key to Understanding the Chapter
   1. v. 32 — Normally in parabolic constancy, the fig tree refers to the nation Israel. "When Israel is yet a young nation, you know the time is near." Israel became a nation again in 1948!
   2. v. 33 — Notice: "ALL these things." All these signs will be prevalent as we approach the end; false christs, false prophets, increased earthquakes, etc.

I. Verses 36-41 — This is Known as a "Rapture Parable"
   1. You can always tell a "Rapture Parable" because it will mention something about not knowing the day or hour. See Verse 36.

J. Verses 42-51 — Another Rapture Parable
1. Jesus sums up His discourse with Rapture Parables (see also 25:1-13, note: v. 13).
2. We don't know the day the Church will be raptured. We do know the exact day of Christ's return at Armageddon, however. See Daniel 12:11. From the time the Antichrist moves his image into the holy Temple in Jerusalem, there will be 1,290 days until Jesus returns. Therefore, the Rapture is a secret event. No man knows the day or hour. It will happen suddenly!

VI. KEY TO UNDERSTANDING THE SIGNS OF THE TIMES
A. See Matthew 24:8 — All These Signs of Which Jesus Spoke are the Beginning of Birth Pangs
1. Only when birth pangs (pains) become more frequent and more intense does it mean that DELIVERY DAY is coming quickly.
2. So when these signs become increasingly frequent and more intense, you'll know the time is near!

3

RELIGIOUS DECEPTION

TEXTS: Matthew 24:4-5   Mark 13:5-6
         Luke 21:8   I Timothy 4:11
         2 Timothy 4:3-4   2 Peter 2:1
         Revelation 13:13-14

BIRTH PAIN Nº 1: WIDESPREAD RELIGIOUS DECEPTION

I.   INCREASING INTENSITY & FREQUENCY OF RELIGIOUS
     DECEPTION AND OCCULTIC REVOLUTION
     A. New Testament Support Scriptures:
        1 Timothy 1:4-7   Colossians 2:8, 18-19
        1 Timothy 4:1-2   2 Thessalonians 2:8-12
        2 Timothy 4:3-4   2 Timothy 3:5
        2 Peter 2:1-2   1 John 2:18
        Galatians 1:8   1 John 4:1
        Romans 16:17-18   2 John 1:9-10
        2 Corinthians 11:3-4   Jude 4
        2 Corinthians 11:12-15   Revelation 13:13-14
        Revelation 16:14

II. THERE HAVE ALWAYS BEEN OCCULTISTS AND OTHER
     DECEIVERS
     A. Magicians (Occultists) Exodus 7:11, 8:7, 18; Daniel 2:27

     B. Simon the Sorcerer (Acts 8)

     C. Elymas the Sorcerer (Acts 13:8)

     D. Girl with a Spirit of Divination (Acts 16:16-18)

     E. False Prophets (1 John 4:2)

     F. This is Not Unusual!

4

III. BUT THE UNUSUAL THING IS THAT FALSE RELIGIONS AND PRACTICES WILL SUDDENLY BEGIN TO MULTIPLY AS WE APPROACH THE SECOND COMING OF CHRIST.
A. "Deceive" (Gr. *Planao*) = To lead or seduce into error. To lead astray.
1. False cults are growing in numbers and in variety.
2. There is a widespread fascination with the preternatural and occult.
3. Spiritualism, palm reading, tarot cards, ouji boards, horoscopes.
4. Satan worship is rampant — Nearly 100 centers in USA alone.
5. TV shows, films, music, cartoons — signs of occult.
6. Ordaining homosexuals common practice now in liberal churches.
7. Junior high and high school fascination with seances.
8. Occultic bookstores are popping up, even in Michigan!
9. Many are departing from the faith.
10. World Council of Churches (liberal) seeks false unity among churches.

IV. ANOTHER DANGEROUS RELIGIOUS DECEPTION THAT WILL INFILTRATE THE CHURCH: UNCONDITIONAL ETERNAL SECURITY! (1 Cor. 6:9-11)
A. St. Paul Said, "Be NOT Deceived...."
1. The following classes of people have NO PART in the Kingdom; they DO NOT have eternal life abiding in them:
   a. Fornicators (those who participate in illicit sex)
   b. Idolaters (those who put anything before God)
   c. Adulterers (those involved in extramarital sex)
   d. Effeminate (homosexuals)
   e. Abusers of themselves with mankind (those who are not homosexuals, but still participate in homosexual activity; bisexuals would fall into this class)
   f. Thieves (cheaters or swindlers)
   g. Covetous (greedy graspers; materialistic-minded)
   h. Drunkards
   i. Revilers (those who slander innocent people)
   j. Extortioners
      1. NONE OF THESE HAVE ANY INHERITANCE IN THE KINGDOM OF GOD.

5

2. St. Paul amplifies in Galatians 5:19-21 and tells us that these will have no share in the Kingdom either:
   a. Lascivious (those eager for lustful pleasure)
   b. Sorcery (AMPL.: illicit use of drugs — enchanting drugs)
   c. Heretics (those who adhere to false doctrine)
   d. Murderers
   e. Those involved in wild parties — disco dancing, etc.

3. Fruit of Eternal Security Doctrine:
   a. Leading many on the road to hell.
   b. In Canada — nude plays in church depicting do-it-yourself abortion.
   c. Ordaining homosexuals as "ministers."
   d. Texas church sponsored a stripper for youth group.

CONCLUSION

A. Jesus Warned Us Ahead of Time and Told Us to "Take Heed!"

B. How to Avoid the Deception Trap:
   1. John 8:31-32 — Continue in the WORD.
   2. Romans 16:17-18 — Beware of those that cause divisions in the Church.
   3. 2 Cor. 11:1-3 — Maintain a sincere devotion to Christ.

C. Here is a Special Excerpt from the *Life For Laymen* Magazine, "Time With Him":
   How can you, as a Christian, discern a "false teacher?" It is most important that you and I know the difference between Truth and false doctrine, for God's people can perish because of the lack of knowledge. Here are 10 Scriptural rules to help us check out a false teacher:
   1. Rebellion against truth (1 Timothy 6:3).
   2. Pride (verse 4).
   3. Ignorance of truth (verse 4).
   4. Doting (exhibiting excessive foolishness) over questions of the law (verse 4).
   5. Debatings - splitting hairs (verse 4).
   6. Envyings - sour tempers (verse 4).
   7. Strife over doctrine (verse 4).

8. Suspicions (verse 4).
9. Evil speakings (verse 4).
10. Seeking personal gain (verse 5).

How are we to treat false teachers? 1 Timothy 6:5 tells us to "withdraw thyself." Jesus told us there would be false teachers in the last days, but we do not need to be taken in by them, for the Word of God can instruct us in Truth.

BIBLE PROPHECY SERIES
STUDY NOTES BY DAVE WILLIAMS

LESSON 3:
Preliminary Signs

PRELIMINARY SIGNS

TEXTS: Matthew 24:3-8, 36-39   Luke 21:9-11
2 Timothy 3:1-5   2 Peter 2:1-22
Genesis 6:1-8

MORE BIRTH PAINS THAT WILL INTENSIFY, INDICATING THE RETURN OF JESUS CHRIST.

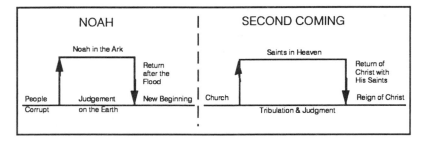

I. **PRELIMINARY SIGNS**
    A. Matthew 24:3-8
        1. Wars
        2. Rumors of Wars
        3. Commotions (see Luke 21:9)
        4. Famines
        5. Epidemics
        6. Earthquakes

II. **MORE PRELIMINARY SIGNS**
    A. In the Days of Noah (Matt. 24:36-39; Genesis 4, 5 & 6)
        1. Population explosion
        2. Materialism and sensuality
        3. Increased demonic activity
        4. Technological explosion

8

5. Building of great cities
6. Violence
7. Abnormal emphasis on sex
8. Marrying and giving in marriage (divorce rate extremely high)
9. Hardness to God's message (2 Peter 2:5, Genesis 6:3)

CONCLUSION:

"WHAT MANNER OF PERSONS OUGHT YE TO BE?"

A. <u>Spiritual (Noah found grace in the eyes of the Lord)</u>

B. <u>Practical and Diligent</u>

BIBLE PROPHECY SERIES
STUDY NOTES BY DAVE WILLIAMS

LESSON 4:
18 Preliminary Signs of Christ's Soon Return

18 PRELIMINARY SIGNS OF CHRIST'S SOON RETURN

TEXTS: Matthew 24   Mark 13
              Luke 21   Genesis 4,5,6
              Psalm 102   Ezekiel 38-39

- ❑ 1. World Focus on the Middle East.
- ❑ 2. Religious deception and occultic revolution.
- ❑ 3. Wars.
- ❑ 4. Rumors of wars.
- ❑ 5. Commotions (chaos politically, socially, economically, etc.)
- ❑ 6. Famines in various parts of the world (hunger).
- ❑ 7. Epidemics (diseases, plagues, insect problems).
- ❑ 8. Earthquakes in various parts of the world.
- ❑ 9. Population explosion.
- ❑ 10. Materialism and sensuality (see theater ads).
- ❑ 11. Increased demonic activity.
- ❑ 12. Great technological advances.
- ❑ 13. People moving to cities.
- ❑ 14. Violence and terrorism.
- ❑ 15. Abnormal emphasis on sex.
- ❑ 16. Family problems will multiply, divorces, etc.
- ❑ 17. Hardness to God's message (mockers, scoffers).
- ❑ 18. Genuine Holy Ghost Revival!

When these signs begin to intensify and accelerate, you'll know that
the end of this age is drawing near.

INGATHERING HARVEST AND THE GLEANING

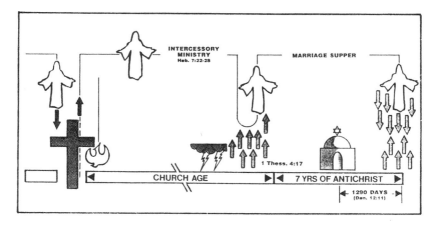

CHART DISPLAYING THE VARIOUS RESURRECTIONS INCLUDED IN THE "FIRST RESURRECTION."

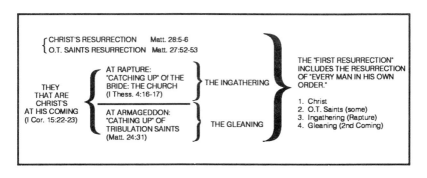

11

"THE BLESSED HOPE" or "THE FIRST FRUIT HARVEST"

TEXTS:

I Thessalonians 4:13-18	John 14:1-3
I Corinthians 15:22-26	I John 2:28
I Corinthians 15:50-58	I John 3:2-3
Titus 2:13	Philippians 3:20-21
Hebrews 11:5	Colossians 3:4
Luke 21:35-36	Matthew 24:36-51
Revelation 3:10	Matthew 25:1-13

WORDS: "CAUGHT UP" (1 Thess. 4:17)
Greek = *harpazo*: "to be snatched up with great force"
Latin Vulgate = *raptus*, where we get the word "rapture"

"LAST TRUMP" (1 Cor. 15:52)
"Assembly call." Not to be confused with the 7th trumpet
of judgment found in the Revelation.

IMPORTANT END TIME EVENTS:
1. Israel is established as a nation (Psalm 102).
2. The preliminary signs begin to accelerate and intensify.
3. Russia becomes increasingly involved in the Middle East
(order the tape, "The Coming Russian Invasion" for a
detailed study).
4. Rapture (the ingathering of the first fruits — the Church).
5. Antichrist unveiled (a world leader arrives on the scene).
6. Tribulation period begins.
7. Rapture ("gleaning" of tribulation saints and elect of Israel
at Armageddon).
8. 1000-year reign with Christ!

EXPERIMENT:
Take 18 large envelopes and label each with a different "sign" of Christ's Return. Clip news articles for an entire year, placing each in their respective labeled envelopes. The results will be astounding and startling!

I. **WHAT IS MEANT BY "RAPTURE?"**
   A. "Caught Up with a Great Force."

   B. This is the Catching Away of True Believers (first fruits) before the Great Tribulation Period.

   C. We will receive new bodies at this time.
      1. Equipped for the universe! (1 Cor. 15:51-58; 1 John 3:2)

II. **DIFFERENT THEORIES CONCERNING THE "RAPTURE"**
   A. Pre-tribulation Rapture*

   B. Mid-tribulation Rapture

   C. Post-tribulation Rapture

   * D. Why I Believe in a Pre-Tribulation Rapture for the Church:
      1. There are different orders (ranks) to the resurrections and rapture(s) (see 1 Cor. 15:22-26). THESE ARE ALL PART OF THE FIRST RESURRECTION.
         a. Christ & many O.T. saints (Matt. 27:52-53, 28:5-6)
         b. Rapture of Church (1 Thess. 4:16-17; Rev. 3:10; Luke 21:35-36)
         c. 144,000 Jewish "evangelists" (Daniel 12:1; Rev. 12:5, 14:1-5)
         d. The two tribulation witnesses (Rev. 11:7-11)
         e. The final gleaning (Tribulation saints & elect Jews) (Matt. 24:31)
      2. Promise in Revelation 3:10 to be kept "from" the hour of temptation (tribulation).
      3. Luke 21:36 must be read in context with Great Tribulation. Pray to escape it!
      4. Pre-tribulation rapture is the only way Christ's return could be imminent.
         a. See Daniel 12:11; Mark 13:35-37; Matthew 24:36, 42,44; 25:13

III. **WHAT IS THE PURPOSE OF THE RAPTURE?**
   A. Provides Sincere Christians an Escape (Luke 21:36) from God's Hour of Wrath.
      1. It is a blessed hope (Titus 2:13).
      2. It is to be comforting (1 Thessalonians 4:18).
      3. God delivered Lot and Noah BEFORE His judgment fell. His character hasn't changed through the years.

   B. The Rapture Provides a Purifying Effect on Believers (1 John 3:2-3)
      1. Expect His return at any time now.
      2. Worldliness drives out spiritual perception and preparedness.

   C. The Rapture Provides a Means of Extracting the Preserving Quality in the Earth so that the Wicked One can be Revealed.
      1. 2 Thessalonians 2:1-7 - Holy Spirit influence will be withdrawn with the Church gone.

   D. The Rapture Will Provide a Means for the Jews to Make Up for Lost Time in Getting God's Message to the World.

IV. **WHAT WILL BE THE EFFECT OF THE RAPTURE ON THE WORLD?**
   A. People Will Rationalize It Away.

   B. Antichrist Forces Will Somehow Neutralize Its Effect.

   C. Nominal Church Members Will Probably Not Believe What Happened.
      1. They may send out "search parties" as was done for Elijah when he was supernaturally transported to heaven.

   D. Others Will Do Some Real Soul-Searching and Confessing of Sins.
      1. See parable of the five foolish virgins (Matt. 25:1-13).

V. **HOW MAY ONE PARTICIPATE IN THE RAPTURE OF THE "FIRST FRUITS?"**
   A. Prepare
      1. Matthew 24:44-51
      2. Amos 4:12

B. Watch and Pray
   1. Luke 21:34-36
   2. Hebrews 9:28

C. Be Patient
   1. 2 Peter 3:3-4,9
   2. James 5:7-8

D. Be a Philadelphian
   1. Revelation 3:7-13
      a. Have love for the brethren
      b. Be mission-minded
      c. Be a soul-winner
      d. Keep the patience of God's Word

PAVING THE WAY FOR THE ANTICHRIST

INTRO: It's interesting to watch the events that God spoke about hundreds of years ago take place in our world today. Never in my life have I felt a greater urgency to proclaim the SECOND COMING of our Lord Jesus Christ as I feel right now. I believe the world is now living on "borrowed time."

REVIEW: 1.   Accelerating signs in the earth.
2.   The "snatching away" of true believers.
3.   The unsuccessful Russian invasion of Israel.

TEXTS: 2 Thessalonians 2:1-12
Verse 1 -   Notice distinction between two events: 1) Second coming; 2) Our gathering.
Verse 2 -   Don't be disturbed by prophecies, rumors, or phony letters telling you that the Tribulation has begun or Second Coming (at Armageddon) is near.
Verse 3 -   Two things will happen before the Second Coming: 1) Religious Apostasy will occur; 2) The man of sin (Antichrist) will be revealed to the world.
Verse 4 -   Antichrist will claim to be God (this will take place 3-1/2 years after he comes into power).
Verse 5 -   REMEMBER, I told you! (We have a tendency to forget so easily.)
Verse 6 -   Something (or someone) is withholding the revelation of Antichrist.
Verse 7 -   "Mystery of Iniquity" = the <u>hidden</u> principle of rebellion against genuine authority.
"Letteth" = restrains. NOTE: The Holy Spirit is now restraining the system of Antichrist, but soon He'll be taken out of the way; not out of the

world. Perhaps when the Church is evacuated, the Holy Spirit's restraining power through the Church will be removed.

Verse 8 - THEN - after the Church is gone and the restraining power of the Holy Spirit is taken out of the way, that "Wicked" Antichrist shall appear. Parenthetical phrase ("whom the Lord shall consume....").

Verse 9 - The Antichrist will be filled with satanic power. He will perform signs and lying wonders. He will be a master of deceit.

Verse 10 - Many will perish under Antichrist's reign because they rejected the Gospel Truth when it was presented.

Verse 11 - They will be deluded and will believe Antichrist's lies and accept them as the truth.

Verse 12 - Their fate: damnation. Because 1) they believed not the truth; 2) they took great pleasure in doing their unrighteous deeds.

I. NAMES OF ANTICHRIST
A. Antichrist (1 John 2:18)

B. The Little Horn (Daniel 7:8,24; 8:9,23)

C. The Prince That Shall Come (Daniel 9:26-27)

D. The Man of Sin (2 Thess. 2:1-12)

E. The Son of Perdition (2 Thess. 2:1-12)

F. That Wicked (2 Thess. 2:8-12; Isa. 11:4)

G. The Beast (Daniel 7:11; Revelation 13)

II. HIS POLITICAL RULE
A. Will Begin in a Ten-Nation Federation in Western Europe. He'll overthrow three, the other seven will voluntarily submit to his leadership (Daniel 7:24; Rev. 17:8-17).

B. Eventually, All the Nations of the World Will Submit Their Authority to This Man. It may be voluntary or of necessity (Rev. 13:7).

III. ANTICHRIST'S RELIGION
   A. He Will Start Out Tolerant of All Religions, including
      Judaism. In fact, he will somehow be affiliated (perhaps
      even remotely) with a great melting pot of all the world
      religions. This is at the beginning of his reign (see Rev.
      17 and Daniel 12).

   B. But Actually, He Will Worship the "God of Forces." He
      will be somehow involved with black magic, or occultism,
      or metaphysical teachings (Daniel 11:38, Daniel 8:23).

   C. He Will Be Empowered by Satan Himself! (Daniel 8:24, 2
      Thess. 2:9, Rev. 13:2).

   D. He Will Desire to be Worshipped as God and Will Move
      His Image into the Holy of Holies in Jerusalem. (Daniel
      12:11, Matt. 24:15, 2 Thess. 2:4, Rev. 13:15)

   E. He Will Have a Powerful "Promotion Agent" Known in
      Prophecy as the False Prophet. (See Rev. 13:11-15.)

IV. ANTICHRIST'S PERSONALITY AND POLICIES
   A. He Will be a Military Genius (Daniel 8:24, Rev. 13:4).

   B. He Will Win Many People (especially working class)
      Through Worthless Promises and Flattery (Daniel
      11:21,23,32).

   C. He Will Rise to Power on a Program of Peace and Security
      (1 Thess. 5:3).

   D. He Will Take Wealth from the Rich and Scatter it Among
      the People. This system of Marxism works only tempo-
      rarily. It's the big businesses and the prosperous people
      that create jobs, etc. Without free enterprise, you can
      scatter the wealth among the poor, but the poor will just use
      it up, never learning how to replace it for themselves.
      (Daniel 11:24)

   E. He Will Cause the People of the World to Use His Mark, or
      His Name, or the Number of His Name (666) In Order to
      Buy or Sell or Receive Any Services Such as Hospitaliza-
      tion, etc. (Rev. 13:16-18; 14:9-11; 16:2; 19:19-20)

F. He Will Possess a Very Magnetic Personality (Daniel 8:23; 11:21-23,32).

G. People Will Find Him Intriguing and Will be Glad to Worship Him (Rev. 13:4).

V. WORLD CONDITIONS AT ANTICHRIST'S RISE
   A. Perplexing (Seemingly Unsolvable) World Problems (Luke 21:25)
      1. Social and moral problems (Daniel 8:23, "...when they have become morally rotten")
      2. Political
      3. Economic
      4. Military and security
      5. Religious problems
      6. The world will be in a state of extreme turmoil!

   B. Anti-Semitism Will Accelerate (Zech. 12:3)
      1. The Antichrist will feign friendship with Israel and will make a peace treaty with Israel that will last only 3-1/2 years (Daniel 9:27, 12:11; Matt. 24:15).

   C. Russia Will Be Defeated as a Military Power (Ez. 38-39)

   D. The United States will have Lost Her Power and Influence in the World

   E. A Powerful Ten-Nation Federation will be the Final World Power (Daniel 2, 7, 8).
      1. Part of old Roman Empire. In fact, it will be sort of a revived Roman Empire.
      2. Bible scholars at the turn of the century were predicting this ten-nation federation in Western Europe. In 1957, the Common Market was formed consisting of six nations. In 1972, three more nations were admitted. In 1981, a tenth nation was accepted. All ten were once part of the old Roman Empire.

CONCLUSION:
   TIME IS RUNNING OUT. BELIEVE THE TRUTH OF JESUS CHRIST BEFORE IT'S TOO LATE!

BIBLE PROPHECY SERIES
STUDY NOTES BY DAVE WILLIAMS

LESSON 7:
The Nations Lining Up On Schedule!

THE NATIONS LINING UP ON SCHEDULE!

TEXT: Luke 21:28-33

BASIC OUTLINE:
I. EUROPEAN NATIONS (THE COMMON MARKET)
II. THE NATION ISRAEL
III. RUSSIA AND HER ALLIES
IV. THE UNITED STATES

I. **THE EUROPEAN NATIONS**
   A. Revelation 13:1; Daniel 2:41-43; Daniel 7:7-8,24

   B. Bible Scholars Have Been Predicting the Rise of a Ten-Nation European Federation
      1. 1957 — The European Economic Community was formed. It included: France, Italy, Belgium, Luxembourg, West Germany, Netherlands.
      2. 1972 — Ireland, Denmark, England admitted (making it nine nations).
      3. 1981 — Greece accepted!

II. **RUSSIA AND HER ALLIES**
    A. Will Make an Unsuccessful Attempt at Invading Israel! (Ezekial 38-39).
       1. Gog, Magog, Meshech, Tubal all refer to the area now occupied by the Soviet Union!
       2. Persia = Iran
       3. Ethiopia = Modern Black African Nations
       4. Libya = United Arab Nations
       5. Gomer = Eastern Slovakian Nations
       6. Togarmah = Armenia
       7. When will it occur? (Ez. 38:8)

III. **ISRAEL** (The Russian invasion will apparently occur when Israel is under worldwide criticism — see Zech. 12:2-3).
   A. Israel Will Fear Further Invasion and Make a Peace Treaty/Covenant with the Antichrist and His Ten-Nation Confederacy (Daniel 9:27).
      1. Isaiah 28:15-16,18 - "covenant with hell"

IV. **THE UNITED STATES** (No direct reference in Bible Prophecy)
   A. Possibilities
      1. Become a dependent satellite of E.E.C.
      2. Nuclear exchange brings destruction (Ex. 39:6)
      3. Fall through cut-off of oil supplies.
      4. REVIVAL!!!
         a. Keys: Pray (2 Chr. 7:14), Assemble (Heb. 10:25), Faith (Luke 18:8), Missions (Rev. 3:10), Share (Matt. 28:19, Acts 1:8)

BIBLE PROPHECY SERIES
STUDY NOTES BY DAVE WILLIAMS

LESSON 8:
The Great Tribulation: An Overview

THE GREAT TRIBULATION: AN OVERVIEW

TEXTS: Daniel 12:1
           Daniel 9:24-27
           Matthew 24:21-22

DANIEL'S 70 WEEKS

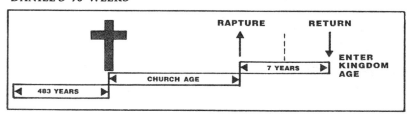

I.   NAMES FOR THE FINAL SEVEN YEARS
      A. Great Tribulation (Matt. 24:21, Rev. 7:14)

      B. Time of Trouble (Daniel 12:1)

      C. Time of Jacob's Trouble (Jer. 30:7)

      D. Hour of Temptation (Rev. 3:10)

      E. Great and Terrible Day of the Lord (Joel 2:31)

      F. Daniel's 70th Week (Daniel 9:24-27)

      G. Day of Trouble and Distress (Zeph. 1:15)

II.   WHEN WILL TRIBULATION OCCUR CHRONOLOGICALLY?
      A. After the Rapture of the Church (Rev. 4:1 - "After these
         things....")

      B. After Russia is Ruined Militarily.

C. The 7-Year Tribulation Will Officially Begin When the Antichrist Makes a Treaty/Covenant with the Nation Israel (Daniel 9:27).

III. **FIRST 3-1/2 YEARS**
   A. Great World Leader Arises with Power and Magnetism.

   B. He Brings Peace and Security to the World in General; Middle East in Particular. Communism Will Be Off the Scene as a Super-Power.

   C. World Leader (Antichrist) Will Receive a Fatal Wound (Perhaps Assasination Attempt) and It Will be Healed and He Will Rise, Astounding the World!

   D. He Will Bring Economic, Political, and Social Stability.

   E. New World Religion (Ecumenical — A Melting Pot) Mixing All Religions Including Occultism!

   F. There Will Be a Growing Hatred Toward Those Christians Left on Earth.

   G. Family Problems, Betrayals Will Plague the World (Luke 21:16; Matt. 24:10).

   H. Rise of Many New False Prophets.

   I. Increase in Sin, Decrease in Natural Affections and Genuine Love.

NOTE: **PREDOMINANT SINS (Rev. 11:8)**
   1. Sexual perversion (figuratively "Sodom")
   2. Religious perversion (figuratively "Egypt")

IV. **FINAL 3-1/2 YEARS**
   A. Antichrist Throws Off His Mask and Reveals His Satanic Nature! (Daniel 9:27)

   B. God's Wrath Will Pour Out Like Never Before!

V. REVELATION SIMPLE OUTLINE
    A. Ch. 1   — Introduction and Key to Understanding

    B. Ch. 2-3   — The Church Age

    C. Ch. 4-5   — Church in Heaven; Earth Getting Ready for
                      Tribulation

    D. Ch. 6-11   — Overview of Tribulation

    E. Ch. 12-14   — Overview of Tribulation, but from Another
                      Angle

    F. Ch. 15-19   — Overview of Tribulation, but from Another
                      Angle Yet

    G. Ch. 20   — Millineum, Final Rebellion, Satan's Doom,
                      Final Judgment

    H. Ch. 21   — New Heaven and New Earth

    I. Ch. 22   — River of Life — Final Invitation and Exhor-
                      tation

VI. OVERVIEW OF TRIBULATION EVENTS
    A. Keep in Mind:
       1. The tribulation will affect the entire earth; however,
          the judgments will occur in different areas of the world
          at different times (usually).
       2. In Revelation, St. John saw two worlds: the spiritual
          and the natural. We must understand how to differen-
          tiate these worlds when reading Revelation.
       3. These are not minute-by-minute predictions. This is not
          a day-by-day schedule; however, all of these events
          WILL happen.

    B. Seals Opened
       1. Rise of Antichrist (Rev. 6:2, Rev. 13)
       2. War, violence, riots (Rev. 6:4)
       3. Famine (Rev. 6:5)
       4. 1/4 of world population dies (Rev. 6:8)
       5. Christians are killed through liquidation programs
          (Rev. 6:9)

6. Great cataclysmic, geophysical occurances (volcanoes, earthquakes, etc.)
7. Great silence in Heaven as prayers are answered (Rev. 8:1-5)

C. Trumpet Judgments
1. Hail, fire, blood — 1/3 of earth burns with fire! (Rev. 8:7)
2. Meteor will plummet into the sea leaving 1/3 ships destroyed and 1/3 of the sea life killed (Rev. 8:8-9).
3. 1/3 of fresh water supplies poisoned (Rev. 8:10).
4. Planet Earth will be darkened by 1/3 (Rev. 8:11-12).
5. Satan opens the Abyss and releases demons which will be allowed to torment people for five months (Rev. 9:13-21).
6. After five months, another 1/3 of the population will die (Rev. 9:20-21).
   a) Still people of the earth will not repent of:
      1. worship of demons (perhaps astrology)
      2. love of silver and gold (covetousness)
      3. murders (abortions)
      4. use of enchanting drugs
      5. sexual immorality and perversions
   b) God would love to forgive and redeem if men would repent.
   c) GOD WILL HAVE TWO WITNESSES IN JERU-SALEM, EXTREMELY POWERFUL (Rev. 11).

D. False Religion and False Science
1. Combining of science and occult

VII. THE CONCLUSION OF THE TRIBULATION PERIOD
A. Economic System of Antichrist Will Fall in One Hour's Time.

B. Earthquakes Will Cause Cities to Completely Fall.

C. Final War Scheduled: Armageddon! (More on this in subsequent lessons.)

D. Jesus Returns on a White Horse.

INVITATION: Revelation 22:17— "COME NOW ALL WHO ARE THIRSTY."

LESSON 9:
The Coming Worldwide Calamities

THE COMING WORLDWIDE CALAMITIES

TEXTS: Matthew 24:21-22 — Jesus tells us of a coming time of unparalleled tribulation.
1. Serious tribulation coming (Matt. 24:21-22)
2. "...no jobs, no wages, no security..." crime rampant (Zech. 8:10 TLB).
3. Top psychics predict a new wave of "peace and prosperity" (1 Thess. 5:3).
4. Recent Russian embarrassments (Ez. 38-39).

REVIEW: Events during the Great Tribulation discussed in Lesson 8:
1. Rise of Antichrist ruler
2. Wars and violence
3. Famine
4. 1/4 population dies
5. Christian liquidation camps
6. Cataclysmic geophysical activity
7. Silence in Heaven for 1/2 hour. Prayers answered.

I.   **MORE CALAMITIES DURING THE FINAL 3-1/2 YEARS**
    A. Revelation 8:7 — Unusual Storms of Hail, Fire and Blood (see also Ez. 38:22).
       1. Could be result of volcanoes, etc.
       2. Illustration: Sign in California classroom: "In the event of earthquake, the Supreme Court's ruling against prayer in school will be temporarily suspended."
       3. Could be from aircraft or perhaps weapons of some sort.
       4. RESULT: 1/3 of the earth's vegetation burns.

    B. Revelation 8:8-9 — A Falling Object Plummets Into the Sea.
       1. Result: 1/3 living creatures in sea die, 1/3 of the ships destroyed.

2. Revelation 16:3 — Eventually the sea will turn to a thick, ill-smelling blood.

C. Revelation 8:10-11 — Huge Falling Star Poisons Water Supplies.
   1. Result: 1/3 of fresh water supply is poisoned.
   2. Revelation 16:4-7 — Eventually the fresh water supplies turn to blood.

D. Revelation 8:12-13 — Planet Earth Darkens by 1/3.
   1. Revelation 16:8-9 — In spite of darkening, people receive sunburns from the ultraviolet rays.
   2. Revelation 16:10-11 — Eventually the entire Antichrist kingdom will fall into a major blackout!
   3. Revelation 16:2 — Sores (ulcers) will break out upon those with the "mark."

E. Revelation 9:1-12 — Satan Opens the Abyss (Place of Incarcerated Spirits).
   1. See Genesis 19:28, Exodus 10:12-15, Exodus 19:18, and Joel 2:10.
   2. Demons are released to vex and torment people for five months. Death impossible.

F. Revelation 9:13-19 — After Five Months 1/3 of Earth's Population Will Die.
   1. Revelation 16:12-16 — Euphrates River dries up in preparation for the kings of the East crossing for Armageddon. Diplomatic demons released.
   2. In spite of all these calamities, people still will not repent (Rev. 9:20-21).
      a) Salvation doesn't count until a person repents!
      b) They refused to repent of:
         1. worshipping devils
         2. covetousness
         3. murders
         4. use of enchanting drugs (sorceries)
         5. sexual immoralities and perversions
         6. thefts
      c) God would love to forgive all who are willing to turn to Him!

G. Revelation 11:15-19 — Transition Complete! Man's
Kingdom Falls and Jesus Prepares to Establish His Literal
Kingdom on Earth!
   1. Revelation 16:17-18 — Loud peals of thunder,
      lightenings and a tremendous earthquake!

II. **WHAT TO DO IN LIGHT OF ALL THIS**
   A. Stay Close to Jesus (Ps. 91:7-8, Matt. 11:28-30, Rev. 22:17)

   B. Stay Close to Christians (Heb. 10:25)

   C. Straighten Out Your Priorities (Col. 3:2)
      1. Three classes of people cannot discern the signs of the
         times:
         a) Hypocrites (Matt. 16:3)
         b) Unconverted who have heard the Gospel, but not
            responded (Matt. 24:38-39)
         c) Those caught up in the "cares of this life!"
            (Luke 21-34)

   D. Get Ready to Leave NOW (Matt. 25).

LESSON 10:
The Battle of Armageddon

THE BATTLE OF ARMAGEDDON

TEXTS: Joel 3:1-2, 9-16   Revelation 19:11-21
Zechariah 14:1-4, 12   Revelation 20:1-3
Revelation 16:12-16

REVIEW: 1. Israel is a nation again under one government (Ez. 37:21-22).
2. Signs of the end begin to intensify (Matt. 24:8)
3. Rapture of the Church (Titus 2:13, 1 Thess. 4:16-17)
4. Rise of Antichrist (Rev. 13, Daniel 7,9,12)
5. Tribulation period with plagues and judgments (Matt. 24:21, Rev. 6-19)
6. Armageddon!

INTRO: WHAT IS ARMAGEDDON?
1. Satan's final strategy of opposition to God's divine program.
2. Final world conflict prior to Christ's return.

I.   **THE PREPARATION FOR ARMAGEDDON**
   A. Revelation 16:12 — Euphrates River Will Dry Up to Permit Kings of the East to Cross.
      1. Already built a dam in Syria capable of doing this.

   B. Revelation 16:13-14 — Spirits of Devils Go Forth to Convince the Nations of the World to Come and Help the Antichrist Annihilate Israel.
      1. Notice the counterfeit trinity:
         a) dragon (Satan)   anti-Father
         b) beast (a man)   anti-Son
         c) false prophet   anti-Spirit
      2. The devils work miracles (lying wonders: 2 Thess. 2:9-10).

3. These deceiving spirits will turn the nations of the world against Israel through their lies and deception (Zech. 14:1-4).

II. **WHERE WILL THIS FINAL CONFLICT TAKE PLACE?**
   A. Valley of Jehoshaphat (Plain of Megiddo)

   B. 2 Chronicles 20 — A Foreshadowing of Armageddon
      1. Receive the report that a coalition of armies is planning to invade.
      2. No chance of survival!
      3. King Jehoshaphat calls the nation to prayer and fasting.
      4. They admit they don't know what to do, but place their lives in God's hands.
      5. A prophet prophesies, "The battle is not yours but the Lord's!"
      6. A great roar of praise and worship goes forth to the Lord.
      7. Israel's enemies are supernaturally wiped out!

III. **ENSUING EVENTS**
   A. The Nations Arrive With Their Armies (Zech. 14:1-2)
      1. Jerusalem raided.
      2. Houses will be ransacked.
      3. Women raped.
      4. 1/2 of the people go into exile.

   B. Strange Sights Begin to Appear in the Skies (Matthew 24:29-30).

   C. Israel Cries Out to God, Finally.

   D. JESUS and the Armies of Heaven on White Horses Come Down from the Eastern Skies (Rev. 19:11-16).

   E. The Elect Jews and Those Who Became Christians During the Tribulation Period will be Gathered Up by Angels. (Many Jews will receive Christ as Messiah.) (Matt. 24:31)

   F. God (Jesus) Will Come and Fight for Israel (Zech. 14:3,5,12; Rev. 19:11-16,19).

IV. **THE FINAL EVENTS**
   A. Zechariah 14:12 and Revelation 19:15 — Utter Devestation to Israel's Enemies.
      1. Revelation 19:17-18,21 — Fowls of the air eat their dead flesh.
      2. Amazing report about the vultures in the Megiddo area. Normally they lay one egg at a time. Strange phenomena: they are now laying 4 eggs at a time! They are multiplying four times faster than usual.

   B. Revelation 19:19-20 — Antichrist and Other World Leaders Try to Make War Against Jesus Himself!
      1. Result: Antichrist and his false prophet will be cast alive into the Lake of Fire!

   C. Zechariah 14:4 — Jesus Will Set Foot on the Mount of Olives!

   D. Zechariah 14:4 — A Great Earthquake Will Occur.

   E. Revelation 20:1-3 — Satan Will be Cast Into the Bottomless Pit! (Praise God!)

   F. Jesus Sets Up His Headquarters in Jerusalem — The World Comes Under a Theocratic Government — Jesus is President of the World!
      1. Revelation 20:1-7
      2. Hosea 3:5
      3. Ezekiel 47 plus many, many more Scriptures will be discussed in a subsequent study.

31

1000 YEARS OF PEACE & PROSPERITY: THE MILLENIUM

TEXTS: Isaiah 2:2-4; 11:6-9
Revelation 20:1-6

I. WHAT IS MEANT BY "MILLENIUM?"
A. Derived From Two Latin Words Meaning "Thousand Years."

B. This 1000-Year Period Will Provide a Time of Theocratic Government Under the Leadership of Jesus Himself.

II. WHEN WILL THE MILLENIUM BEGIN?
A. At the End of Armageddon When the Human Governments of the World Fall.

B. Other Events at This Time:
1. Satan will be bound (Rev. 20).
2. Nations shall be judged (Matt. 25:31-46).
3. A time of rebuilding and reconstruction (Isa. 2:4).

C. The Millenium is Also Known as "The Kingdom Age."
1. Technically we are in a "Kingdom Age" now, in that we can function on Kingdom Principles.
2. But during the millenium, the physical appearing of the Kingdom will come to the earth.

III. WHAT WILL BE THE CONDITIONS DURING THE MILLENIUM?
A. Satan Will Be Bound!
1. Now he's going around the world tempting, deceiving, and hindering all that is good (1 Peter 5:8, 1 Thess. 2:18).

B. Universal Knowledge of the Lord — No Evangelism as We Know It Today.
   1. Zechariah 8:22-23, Isaiah 11:9, Jeremiah 31:34

C. The Government of the World Will be Theocratic (Hos. 3:5, Jer. 30:9, Ez. 37:24, Psalm 48:1-3, Isa. 2:2-4)
   1. Capitol City will be Jerusalem (where Jesus died — now glorified!)
      a) Shekinah Glory will overshadow the city (Ez. 9-10, 43:15; Isa. 4:4-6)
   2. No more voting on candidates or issues. God's will shall prevail.
      a) No adversarial form of government where several men fight for the same job.
      b) Jesus will appoint the leadership on the basis of their faithfulness to the tasks assigned them in this life (Luke 19, Rev. 2:26-27, Daniel 9:27). We will reign on the basis of how faithful we've been to do what God has called us to do.
      c) Righteousness will be enforced (Rod of Iron).

D. Universal Peace Throughout the World (Isa. 2:4, Micah 4:3-4)
   1. No more huge military to support.
   2. Peace even among animals and children (Isa. 11).

E. Longevity Will Be Restored (Isa. 65:20-22, Zech. 8:4).
   1. Survivors of the Tribulation will live to be a ripe old age. A person 100 years old will be considered still a child.

F. Sickness and Disease Will Be a Thing of the Past!

G. No More Severe Storms. Climate Will Be Just Right for Agriculture.

IV. THE END OF THE MILLENIUM
A. Satan Will Be Loosed for Just a Short Season and There Will Be One Final Rebellion. All Who Rebel Will Be Cast into the Lake of Fire.

CONCLUSION: What Will Your Position Be During the Millenium?

LESSON 12:
The Two Judgments

THE TWO JUDGMENTS

MAIN TEXT: Hebrews 9:27

I.   **TWO CLASSES OF HUMAN BEINGS**
    A. SAVED — Those Who Have Repented of Sins, Accepted
      Christ, and Follow Him.

    B. LOST (Damned) — Those Who Do Not Follow Christ.
      1. John 3:16-18
      2. Mark 16:16
      3. Romans 10:9-10

II. **TWO JUDGMENTS**
    A. The Judgment Seat of Christ
      1. Romans 14:9-12
      2. 2 Corinthians 5:8-10
      3. Revelation 11:15-18
      4. WHEN WILL IT OCCUR? During the Great Tribul-
         ation while Christians are in Heaven with the Lord.
      5. PURPOSE:
         a) Not to judge sin (Heb. 10:17, Ez. 33:16, Col. 2:14-15,
           2 Cor. 5:17-21).
         b) Rewards; not judgment for sins (Matt. 10:42).

    B. The Great White Throne Judgment
      1. Revelation 20:11-21:8
      2. WHEN? After the 1000-year reign of Christ on Earth.
      3. WHO WILL BE JUDGED? The lost! All who failed to
         follow Jesus Christ.
         a) Cain — wanted religion on his own terms
         b) Ahab — blamed others for his failures
         c) Balaam — betrayed God's people because of his
           love for money

d) Judas — betrayed Jesus when the going got rough
e) Pilate — a people-pleaser rather than a God-pleaser
f) Demas — forsook the Lord (1 Tim. 4:8-10; see Ez. 18:24)
g) Felix — said he'd call for the preacher at his convenience
h) Agrippa — he was almost persuaded

III. TOO LATE (IF YOU FIND YOURSELF AT THE GREAT WHITE THRONE OF JUDGMENT)
A. Five Emotional Stages to Dying
   1. Denial
   2. Anger
   3. Bargaining
   4. Depression
   5. Acceptance

B. Hell Was Never Prepared for Humans (Matt. 25:41).

C. God has Provided a Means of Escape — Trust in Jesus Christ (Romans 6:23).

CONCLUSION:
A. Which Judgment Will You Attend?

B. Which Words Will You Hear?
   1. "Welcome home, My child. Enter into the joy of the Lord and His Golden City."

   OR
   2. "Depart from me ye cursed, into everlasting punishment, which was prepared for the devil and his demons."

BIBLE PROPHECY SERIES
STUDY NOTES BY DAVE WILLIAMS

BIBLIOGRAPHY

The following is a list of general reference material used in preparing this series on Bible Prophecy:

BOOKS:

Title	Author	Publisher
Dakes Annotated Bible	Finis J. Dake	Dake
Preparing for the Storm	Kenneth Barney	Gospel Publishing
Bible Headlines	Jack Van Impe	Van Impe
The Nations in Prophecy	John F. Walvoord	Zondervan
Late Great Planet Earth	Hal Lindsay	Zondervan
Prophetic Light	Frank M. Boyd	Gospel Publishing
Jesus is Coming	W.E.B.	Revell
Calamity!	D.W. Matter	Old Paths
After the Rapture	W.V. Grant	Grant
The Vision	David Wilkerson	Spire
Racing Toward Judgment	David Wilkerson	Spire
The Second Coming	W.M. Tidwell	Nazarene Publishing
The Second Coming	Gordan Lindsay	C.F.N.
21 Things about Israel	Gordan Lindsay	C.F.N.
End of the Age	Gordan Lindsay	C.F.N.
Revelation	Gordan Lindsay	C.F.N.
666	Salem Kirban	Kirban
Countdown to Rapture	Salem Kirban	Kirban
1000	Salem Kirban	Kirban
Rise of Antichrist	Salem Kirban	Kirban
Christ Returns by 1988	Colin H. Deal	Deal
Israel: Target for Terror	Dan Betzer	Gospel Publishing
Judgment on America	David Wilkerson	Wilkerson
Look Up!	Richard DeHaan	Radio Bible Class
That Blessed Hope	Richard DeHaan	Radio Bible Class
Soon to be Revealed Antichrist	Chuck Smith	Maranatha
Snatched Away!	Chuck Smith	Maranatha
End Times	Chuck Smith	Maranatha
What the World is Coming To	Chuck Smith	Maranatha
Signs of His Coming	Arthur Bloomfield	Bethany

Title	Author	Publisher
Before Armageddon	Arthur Bloomfield	Bethany
God Speaks Today	Gerald Derstine	Gospel Crusade
1980's: Countdown to Armageddon	Hal Lindsay	Bantam
The Trumpet Shall Sound	C.M. Ward	Gospel Publishing
World War III	John Wesley White	Zondervan
50 Questions	Wim Malgo	Midnight Call
What Next!	Kenneth Schmidt	New Hope Press
Prophecy Answered	Keith L. Brooks	Good News
World War III & Destiny of America	Charles R. Taylor	Sceptre
Changing Climate	Arthur Bloomfield	Bethany
Escape from Tribulation	Guy Duty	Bethany
What on Earth's Happening?	Ray Stedman	Regal
Things to Come	Theodore H. Epp	Moody

ABOUT THE AUTHOR

Dave Williams is pastor of Mount Hope Church and International Outreach Ministries with over 4000 regular attenders. On the ministry's scenic 43 acres sits the new multi-million dollar worship and teaching center, designed to comfortably seat over 3000 people. The new complex includes educational facilities, executive offices, a television production center, and world outreach headquarters.

Williams is president of Mount Hope Bible Training Institute, author of 72 audio cassette teaching programs, two leadership video training programs, and has written 27 books, including the seven-time best seller, *The Start of Something Wonderful.* His written articles and reviews have appeared in newspapers and magazines nationwide.

Dave is seen weekly on the television programs, DAVE WILLIAMS AND MOUNT HOPE ALIVE and THE PACESETTER'S PATH. His international speaking ministry has taken him to several nations including parts of Europe, Tanzania, South Africa, and other places of the world.

Dave resides in the Lansing area with his wife, Mary Jo, and their children.

For a complete catalog of books, tapes, videos, and courses by Dave Williams, write to:

Dave Williams
202 South Creyts Road
Lansing, MI   48917

Please include your prayer requests and comments when you write.

FAITHBUILDING BOOKS
by Dave Williams

THE SECRET OF POWER WITH GOD

Here are thirty chapters filled with concise information about prayer that brings results. You'll learn proper prayer management, God's address, the miracle of thanksgiving, how to discern God's will, and "tons" of other helpful "secrets" of power with God.

0-938020-15-3 .... $2.95

THE DESIRES OF YOUR HEART ...
... CAN BECOME REALITIES!

How to Change Your Dreams Into Realities; How to Develop Faith That Works; How to Receive Heaven-sent Ideas; How to Win When Facing Opposition; 15 Causes of Failure and How to Avoid Them; Setting and Reaching Your Goals. 149 pages of practical faith-building material!

0-938020-02-1 .... $2.95

THE CHRISTIAN
JOB-HUNTER'S HANDBOOK

101 pages of practical help for finding the right job — even in a recession! You'll learn how to prepare an effective resume, how to find your calling in life, and how to get the job you want!

0-938020-01-3 .... $3.25

THE NEW LIFE ...
THE START OF SOMETHING WONDERFUL

Our best seller! This book is being used by pastors, evangelists, teachers, and missionaries in many parts of the world. 44 pages of practical, concise guidelines to experiencing a victorious walk with Jesus Christ. The perfect book to give to new convert. QUANTITY PRICES AVAILABLE.

0-938020-03-X $1.95
0-938020-21-8 (Spanish Edition) $1.95

SUCCESS PRINCIPLES
FROM THE LIPS OF JESUS

In this book, Dave Williams shares 10 powerful principles for success in your life. You'll learn how to follow God's guidance, overcome procrastination, accomplish more, and become the pacesetter God wants you to be.

0-938020-00-5 .... $2.95

■ Quantity Discounts Available ■
MOUNT HOPE PUBLICATIONS
202 S. Creyts Rd. ■ Lansing, MI 48917

FAITHBUILDING BOOKS
by Dave Williams

THE ART OF PACESETTING LEADERSHIP

Are you the kind of leader God is looking for? Find out by reading The Art of Pacesetting Leadership — an entire Leadership & Ministry Development course in itself. Taken from Pastor Dave's highly acclaimed "Pacesetting Leadership" class, this book's topics include: Levels of Leadership, Qualities Exhibited in Master-Level Leaders, The Kind of Leader God is Looking For, How to Overcome Stress and Pressure in the Ministry, and so much more. This is perhaps Pastor Williams' most important book.

0-938020-34-X $7.95

THE PASTOR'S PAY

Most church members have little or no knowledge of the concerns, frustrations, and needs of their pastor. Dave Williams, in a gentle, tender way, takes a close look at how much a pastor is worth, who sets his pay, and the scriptural guidelines for paying him. You'll learn the Biblical principles for setting the pastor's pay.

0-938020-36-6 .... $4.95

SLAIN IN THE SPIRIT
IS IT REAL OR FAKE?

What would you think if you saw someone fall, as if dead, to the ground? What if the fall accompanied foaming at the mouth? . . . moaning and groaning? Is it real? Is it fake? This book explains Satanic Manifestations versus God's Visitations, The Supernatural Power and Manifestations of God's Glory, The Purpose of Signs and Wonders, Abuses and Shams, The History of This Phenomenon, Why Some Oppose This Manifestation, and When Does Being Slain in the Spirit Occur.

0-938020-32-3 .... $1.50

GETTING TO KNOW YOUR HEAVENLY FATHER

This book will lead you into that personal relationship with your heavenly Father you so desire. It discusses Christianity as a wonderful and fulfilling family relationship, not merely a religious experience. Find out the difference between theological tradition and the truth of God's character. Also included are Principles For Parents, and How to Claim Your Daily Benefits As a Child of God.

0-938020-35-8 .... $1.50

15 BIG CAUSES OF FAILURE

God did not create you to fail. He created you to succeed and have victory in every area of your life. This Mount Hope micro-book book takes a look at 15 common causes of failure in believer's lives and how to avoid them. You'll also learn how to get on that road to success which God has ordained for your life.

0-938020-13-7 .... $1.00

FAITHBUILDING BOOKS
by Dave Williams

LONELY IN THE MIDST OF A CROWD

Did you know that severe loneliness can cause severe health problems? Some escape routes lead nowhere, but this book by Dave Williams shows the simple two-fold answer to loneliness. You never need to be lonely again.

0-938020-26-9 .... $1.25

7 SIGNPOSTS ON THE ROAD
TO SPIRITUAL MATURITY

Are you maturing spiritually, or have you stalled in your walk with God? This book points out seven sure-fire indicators of spiritual maturity. Learn where you stand now, and where you need to go in order to experience the benefits of a spiritually mature life.

0-938020-29-3 .... $1.50

UNDERSTANDING SPIRITUAL GIFTS

Dave Williams says, "There is no resting point spiritually. We must keep growing and reaching for all that God has for us, or else spiritual paralysis will set in." In this book, an excerpt from *Finding Your Ministry and Gifts*, Pastor Williams concisely explains each spiritual gift and how to function properly in it. A much-needed book for Charismatics and Pentecostals. 32 pages.

0-938020-31-5 .... $1.75

THE REVIVAL POWER OF MUSIC

Does music bring in the glory of God? Dave Williams tells how the tremendous power of God can be released when the song of the Lord comes to His people's hearts. He'll take you on a journey in history, studying great revivals, and how music accompanied them. Does music take commitment? Is it a cure for depression? ... A deliverance from oppression? Learn what the to hindrances to praise and worship are, and how music can bring victory. A Mount Hope micro-book.

0-938020-33-1 .... $1.00

TONGUES AND INTERPRETATION

How would you like to be charged-up with supernatural power from God? You can learn the secret of using your prayer language daily. This micro-book discusses the baptism in the Holy Spirit, the supernatural language, and how you, as a believer, can interpret your supernatural language of the Spirit. Learn the history of speaking in tongues in the Christian church. What did Augustine, Martin Luther, and others say about tongues? Find out, as you read this Mount Hope micro-book, "Tongues and Interpretation."

0-938020-37-4 .... $1.00

■ Quantity Discounts Available ■
MOUNT HOPE PUBLICATIONS
202 S. Creyts Rd. ■ Lansing, MI 48917

FAITHBUILDING BOOKS
by Dave Williams

REMEDY FOR WORRY AND TENSION

Are you bored with life? Do you feel tired . . . run down? If so, you may be suffering from the deadly disease of worry! In this book, Dave Williams shows how you can break loose from the pollution of worry and tension!

0-938020-27-7 .... $1.25

FINDING YOUR MINISTRY AND GIFTS

Find out where you fit in! At last . . . a concise, point-by-point study book defining and describing the ministries and gifts from God. You'll study: personality gifts, charismatic gifts, ministry gifts, supportive gifts, plus much, much more.

0-938020-16-8 .... $5.95

THE GRAND FINALE:
A STUDY ON THE COMING END-TIME REVIVAL

What does the future hold? Will it be revival? Dave Williams says "YES!" This book takes you on a journey into the very near future and describes some of the exciting events just ahead for the Church of Jesus Christ. Find out: How to prepare for the coming revival; What the latter rain will bring; Conditions for revival.

0-938020-18-8 .... $1.75

THE MINISTRY OF
LAYING ON OF HANDS

A guide into a fundamental Bible doctrine. Learn about: imparting blessings, transmitting God's power, administering the Holy Spirit Baptism, revealing or confirming spiritual gifts, and the abuses of this ministry. Dave Williams examines the Bible's answer to this often misunderstood doctrine.

0-938020-23-4 .... $1.75

PATIENT DETERMINATION

Is the Christian life worth all the trouble? Why are there so many problems along the way? *Patient Determination* presents Bible-truths for turning setbacks into victories.

0-938020-24-2 .... $1.00

• Quantity Discounts Available •
MOUNT HOPE PUBLICATIONS
202 S. Creyts Rd. • Lansing, MI 48917

FAITHBUILDING BOOKS
by Dave Williams

FAITH GOALS . . . THE SECRET OF
SETTING AND REACHING THEM

Find out how you can become a peak achiever for God. This book describes how to make plans, set goals and get results. Did you know that only about 5% of all people in America have specific goals, and those who do will achieve 100 to 1000 times more in their lifetime? Faith Goals is an 8-1/2 X 11 inch book, complete with worksheets!

0-938020-04-8 .... $3.95

GENUINE PROSPERITY . . .
A BIBLICAL PERSPECTIVE

High utility bills? Inflation? Rising food costs? If these concern you and your family, you need this book. Dave Williams shares the simple, Scriptural way to get out of debt, clean up your finances, and climb onto the road to complete financial victory.

0-938020-10-2 .... $1.25

HOW TO GET OUT OF
THE TORMENTING CAVE OF DEPRESSION

This micro-book describes in detail what it's like to be depressed, symptoms of depression, its effects, how to recognize the roots of depression, etc. This anointed teaching will show the depressed person how to get out of the tormenting cave of depression, and climb to the peak of "victory mountain."

0-983020-25-0 .... $1.50

GROWING UP IN OUR FATHER'S FAMILY

Learn the Kingdom Keys to Growing up spiritually. You'll study the babyhood, childhood, and mature stages of spiritual growth (Which one are you in?), discover the "master key" to greatness, and discover the amazing benefits of practicing the "extra-miler" principle.

0-938020-11-0 .... $1.25

THE BEAUTY OF HOLINESS

This easily-read book delves into the often ignored and seldom understood topic of holiness. Practical and concise, it teaches what holiness is and what it is not, the advantages of holy living, and how you can follow holiness.

0-938020-22-6 .... $1.25

■ Quantity Discounts Available ■
MOUNT HOPE PUBLICATIONS
202 S. Creyts Rd. ■ Lansing, MI 48917

FAITHBUILDING VIDEO MESSAGES

by Dave Williams

THE PASTOR'S PAY

A motivational one-hour video featuring Dave Williams speaking about the minister's pay. This video will motivate pastors and board members to study, in depth, how God feels about the pastor's pay.

1 Hour Video $12.95

THE UNPARDONABLE SIN
AND THE SIN UNTO DEATH

• Confusion Over the "Unpardonable Sin" • How Can We Understand the Unpardonable Sin • 5 Phases to Committing the Unpardonable Sin • 2 Types of Death • 3 Keys to a Longer Life • Some Who Came Under the Sin Unto Death • Some Who Repented in Time

2 Hour Video $19.95

YOUR GREATEST WEAPON
IN THE STORMS OF LIFE

• A Great Lesson In Faith • The Power of Life is in the Tongue • The Kind of Words Jesus Spoke • How to Speak the Results You Want • Faith Words — Your Greatest Weapon Against the Storms of Life

2 Hour Video $19.95

10 COMMANDMENTS
FOR GUARANTEED FAILURE

• Success or Failure . . . The Choice Is Yours
• 10 Commandments Guaranteed to Make You a Successful Failure . . . OR
• Don't Do These and You'll Succeed

1 Hour Video $12.95

For your convenience, you may order any product listed here by using the form on the following pages.

■ Quantity Discounts Available ■
MOUNT HOPE PUBLICATIONS
202 S. Creyts Rd. ■ Lansing, MI 48917

FAITHBUILDING PRODUCTS
for Pacesetting People by Dave Williams

ORDER FORM

Qty.	Title	Price	Amt.
BOOKS			
____	The A.I.D.S. Plague	1.95	_____
____	Deception, Delusion & Destruction	4.95	_____
____	Supernatural Soulwinning	1.95	_____
____	Somebody Out There Needs You!	1.75	_____
____	End Time Bible Prophecy (Study Notes)	1.75	_____
____	Supernatural Gifts of the Holy Spirit (Study Notes)	1.75	_____
____	The Secret of Power With God	2.95	_____
____	The Christian Job-Hunter's Handbook	3.25	_____
____	The NEW LIFE: The Start of Something Wonderful	1.95	_____
____	The NEW LIFE (Spanish Edition)	1.95	_____
____	Setting & Reaching Your Faith Goals	3.95	_____
____	Genuine Prosperity: A Biblical Perspective	1.25	_____
____	How to Get Out of the Tormenting Cave of Depression	1.50	_____
____	Growing Up in Our Father's Family	1.25	_____
____	You Can Win With Patient Determination (microbook)	1.00	_____
____	The Beauty of Holiness	1.25	_____
____	The Grand Finale: A Study on the Coming End-Time Revival	1.75	_____
____	The Ministry of the Laying On of Hands	1.75	_____
____	Lonely in the Midst of a Crowd	1.25	_____
____	Understanding Spiritual Gifts	1.75	_____
____	The Desires of Your Heart Can Become Realities	2.95	_____
____	Remedy for Worry & Tension	1.25	_____
____	7 Signposts on the Road to Spiritual Maturity	1.50	_____
____	Getting to Know Your Heavenly Father	1.50	_____
____	Revival Power of Music (microbook)	1.00	_____
____	Slain in the Spirit: Is It Real or Fake?	1.50	_____
____	Finding Your Ministry & Gifts	5.95	_____
____	The Art of Pacesetting Leadership	7.95	_____
____	The Pastor's Pay	4.95	_____
____	Tongues and Interpretation (microbook)	1.00	_____
____	15 Big Causes of Failure (microbook)	1.00	_____
____	How to Invest An Hour in Prayer	1.75	_____
____	Success Principles from the Lips of Jesus	2.95	_____
COURSES			
____	The Art of Pacesetting Leadership	69.95	_____
____	Ministry Growth & Development	59.95	_____
____	Your Financial Success	37.95	_____
____	Supernatural Gifts of the Spirit	37.95	_____
____	Successful Church Governments	59.95	_____

AUDIO CASSETTE SETS

____ The Pastor's Pay (2 cassettes)	10.00	_____
____ Relief from Worry & Pressures (3 cassettes)	15.00	_____
____ Spiritual Warfare (12 cassettes)	50.00	_____
____ Fasting for the Impossible (2 cassettes)	10.00	_____
____ The Coming "Grand Finale" Revival (4 cassettes)	20.00	_____
____ The Supernatural Gifts (4 cassettes)	20.00	_____
____ Your Greatest Weapons in the Storms of Life (2 cassettes)	10.00	_____
____ Intercessory Prayer (3 cassettes)	15.00	_____
____ What To Do When You've Lost Your Motivation (2 csts)	10.00	_____
____ End-Times Bible Prophecy (3 cassettes)	15.00	_____

VIDEOS

____ 10 Commandments for Failure	12.95	_____
____ Your Greatest Weapon in the Storms of Life	19.95	_____
____ What To Do When You've Lost Your Motivation	19.95	_____
____ The Art of Pacesetting Leadership (14 sessions)	239.70	_____
____ Ministry Growth & Development (10 sessions)	171.25	_____
____ The Pastor's Pay (1 session)	12.95	_____

TOTAL ORDER $ _____

Please include Payment with Order. Thank You!

DISCOUNT & QUANTITY PRICES: Discount and quantity prices are available for ministers, churches, non-profit organizations, and book stores. Please write to DAVCO COMMUNICATIONS, P.O. Box 80386, Lansing, MI 48917-0386 or telephone (517) 321-2780.

INDIVIDUAL ORDERS: For individual orders, please write to: THE HOPE STORE, 202 S. Creyts Road, Lansing, MI 48917. Tel: (517) 321-2780

Michigan Residents: Please include appropriate sales tax.

Orders are processed immediately upon receipt. Please include full payment with your order. It helps us to serve you better, avoiding C.O.D.s and billings. VISA and MasterCard orders accepted.

PLEASE PRINT CLEARLY

Name _____

Address _____

City _____

State _____   ZIP _____

Please include $1.50 for postage and handling on all orders less than $20.00. Thanks!

VISA _____   MasterCard _____

Expiration Date _____

Signature _____